ODD DOGS

CHAIRMAN OF THE BOARD
SHEBASCO PET FOODS INC.

By the same author

A Hundred and One Uses of a Dead Cat
Unspeakable acts
A Hundred and One More Uses of a Dead Cat
Odd Visions and Bizarre Sights
Success and How To Be One
Teddy
Uniformity
Stroked Through the Covers
Totally U.S.

For children

Tough Ted and Desmond Dougall

SIMON BOND

ODD DOGS

A hundred and one scenes of canine life

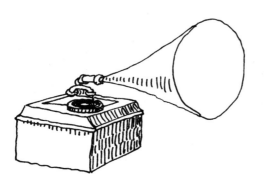

Methuen

First published in 1989
by Methuen London
81 Fulham Road, London SW3 6RB
Copyright © Simon Bond 1989

British Library Cataloguing in Publication Data
Bond, Simon, *1947–*
    Odd dogs: 101 scenes of canine life.
    1. English humorous cartoons
    – Collections from individual artists
    I. Title
    741.5'942

    ISBN 0–413–19290–3

Printed in Great Britain
by Richard Clay Ltd, Bungay, Suffolk

'Oh my God, dog biscuits are down!'

'And in lane four, representing Battersea Dogs Home . . .'

CANINE PHILOSOPHY

THE WORD BATH IS MENTIONED

BEYOND THE CALL OF DUTY

'Oh yes, occasionally he's very boisterous.'

A GREAT DANE IN THE THROES OF FURIOUS ACTIVITY

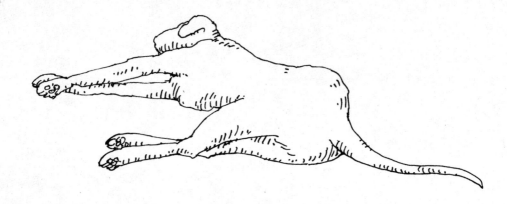

THE LONE RANGER
AND FIDO

'Forget it . . . just black coffee'

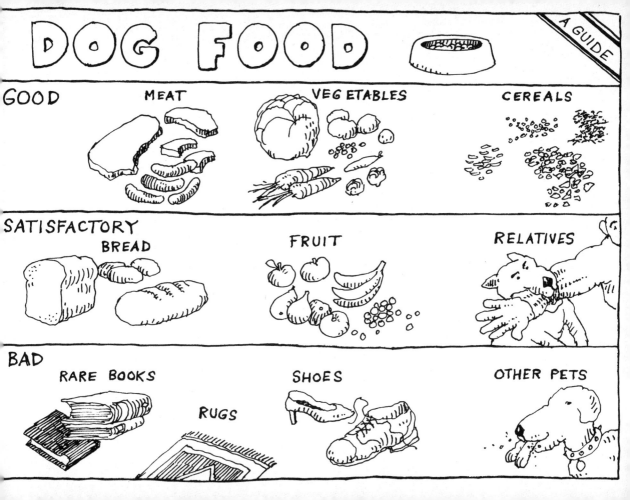

A POINTLESS CONVERSATION

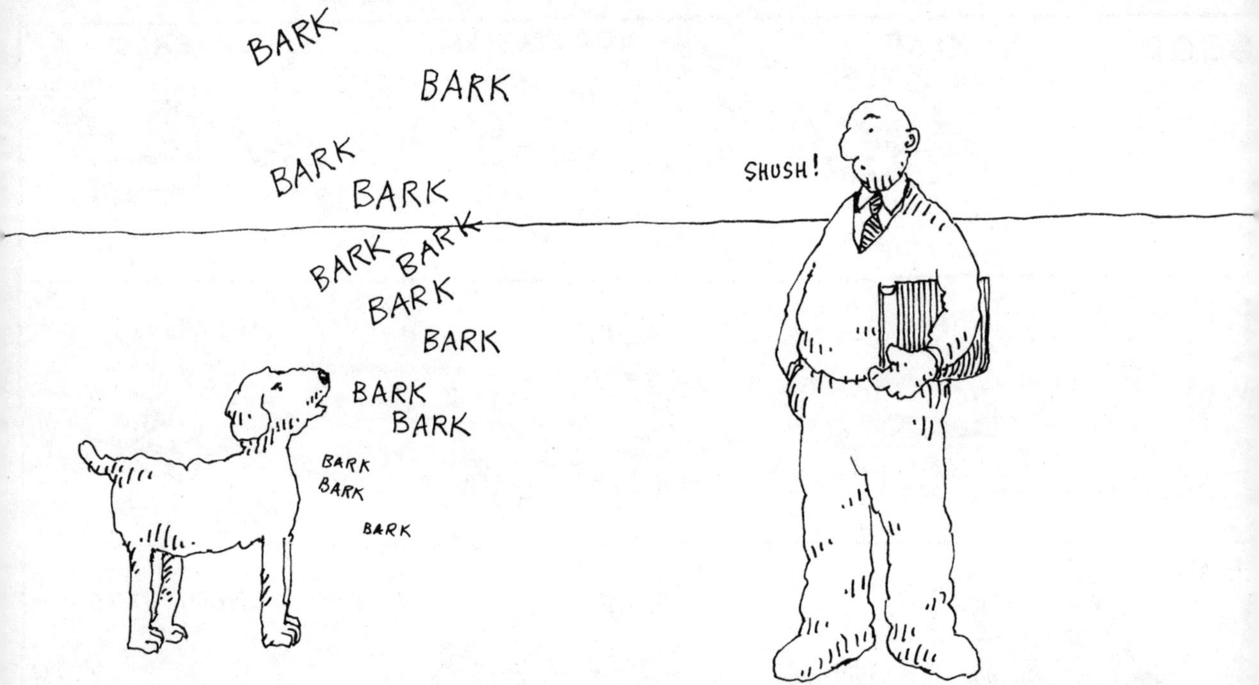

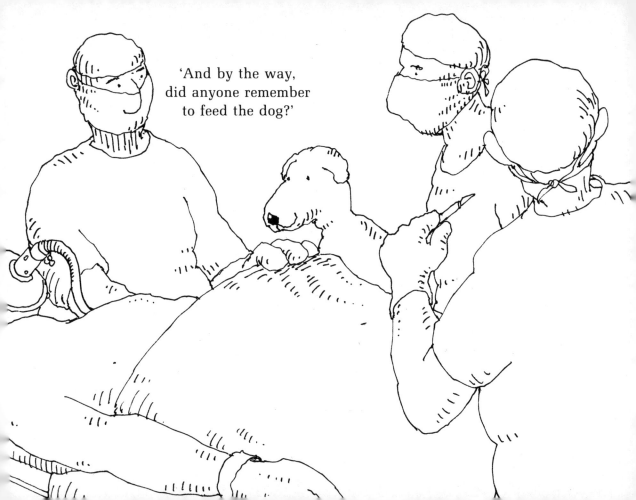

KNOW YOUR DOG

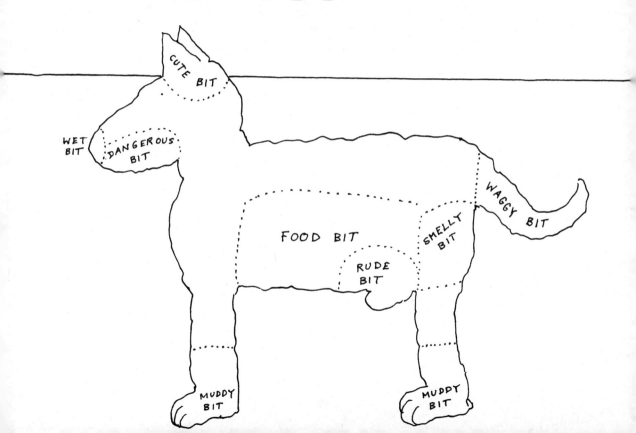

DOWN IN THE FOREST
NOTHING STIRRED...

'Lord and Lady
Lascelles de Vere Digby
and their ratty
little mongrel, Tinker.'

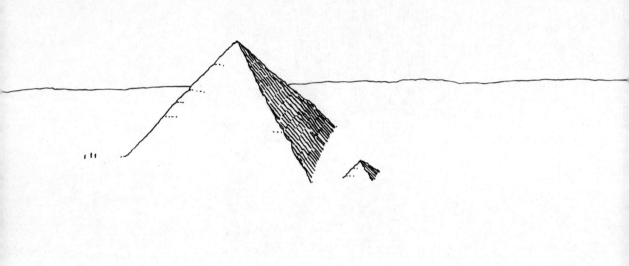

'Oh Rex, can we really afford it?'

'Singing and dancing no problem . . . but I don't do nude scenes.'

'Margie, this dog's got to go ... he's just too cute!'

DONNY — A DOG OF THE 80'S

Of course you have a choice. You can have it in your bowl... or on the floor.... what's it to be, Mister Choosey?

THE FIRST MESS

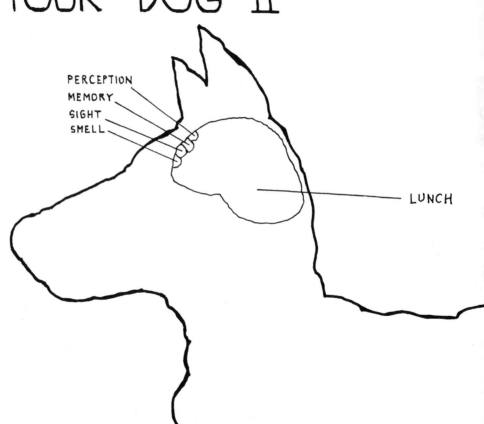

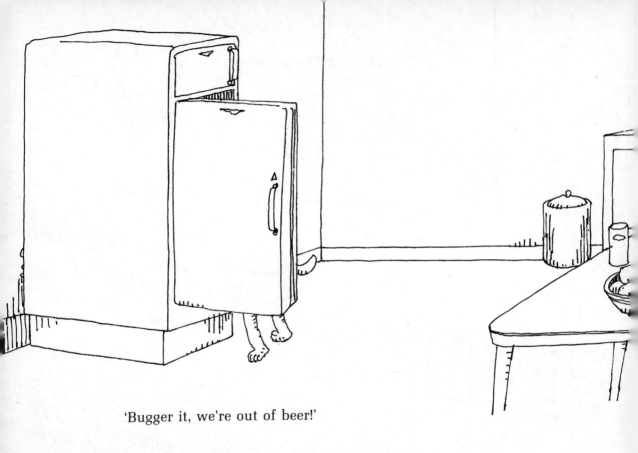

'Bugger it, we're out of beer!'

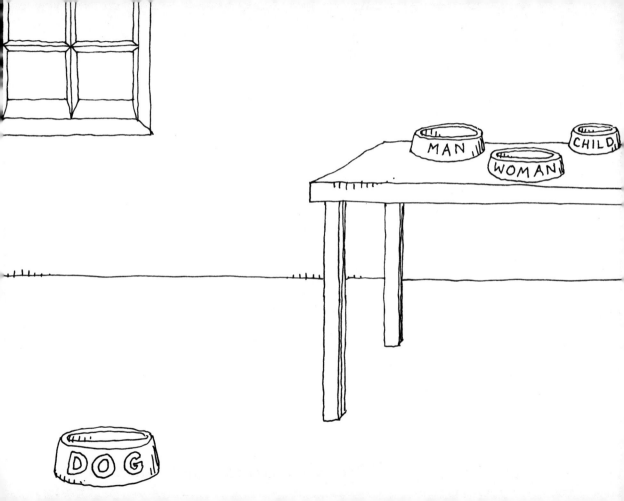

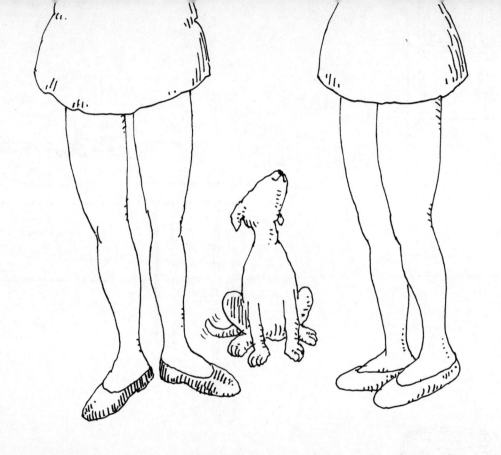

SCOTTY — THE DOG WHO LOVED MINI-SKIRTS

'Oh yes, he's wonderfully obedient.'

'And who ordered the dry martini with a dash of liver?'

'Katherine, why can't he eat like other dogs?'

'Are you stupid – it's pouring down!'

'Alice, apparently I'm taking King for a walk.'

'Well, if a dog's going to beg, that's the way to do it.'

'And when you want
to go to the toilet
would you please bark.'

The Sophisticate

THE HOUND OF THE BASKETBALLS

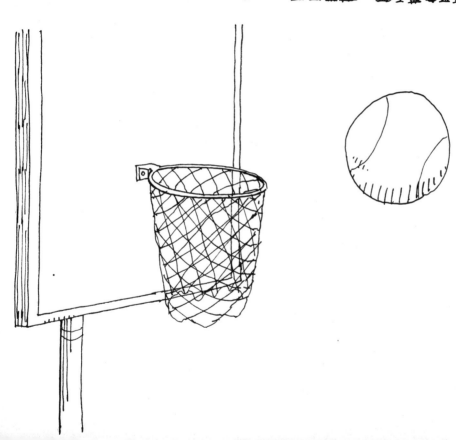

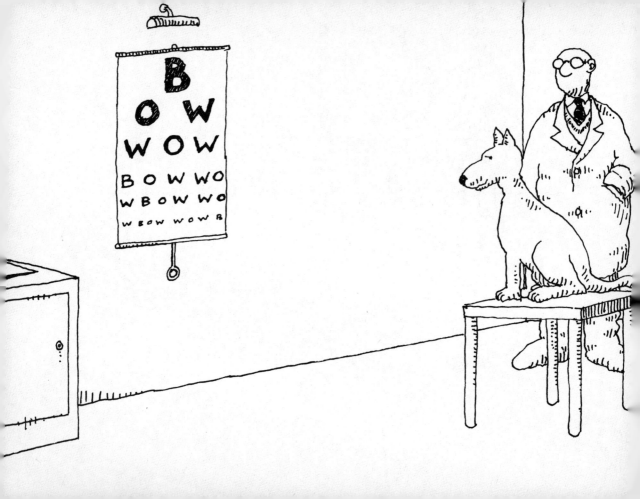

'He's about five ten . . .
dark brown hair . . . slim . . .'

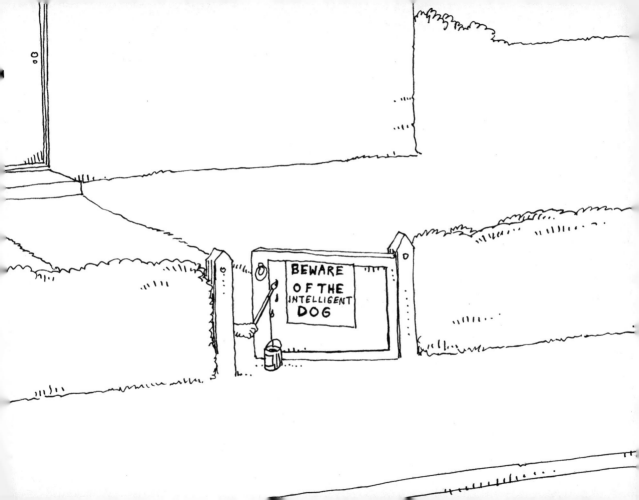

MAY 1939   The Germans Invade Poland (Surreptitiously)

16

WARNING

MINIATURE
POODLES
ON HEAT

PLEASE PROTECT

YOUR ANKLES

STICKS AVAILABLE

'If he misses, can I have the apple?'

IRONY

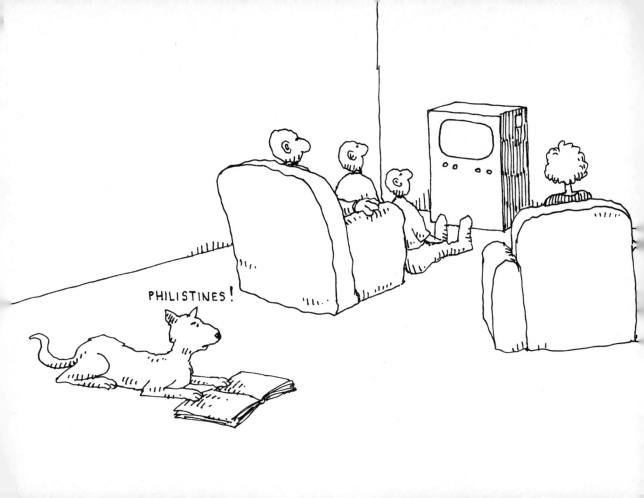

'Jesus! I thought mine was bad.'

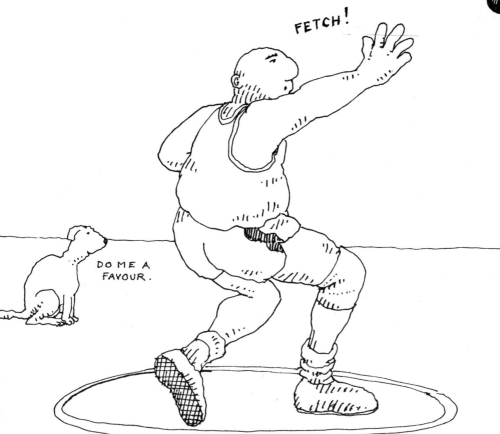

'Just where the hell have you been, I've been worried sick!'

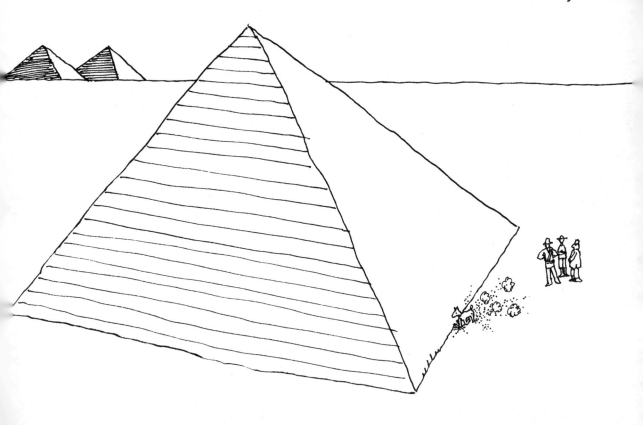

THE TUTANKHAMEN EXPEDITION 1908 (The Economy Version)

'Rusty, do it like everyone else, will you!'

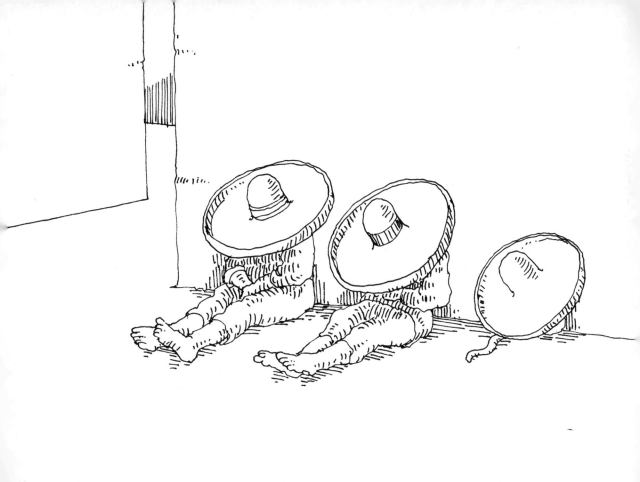

'Forgive me father,
for I have sinned . . .
I ate a paperback and
pee-ed on the carpet.'

NERO
Hero of the
Fire Service

MAC
OF THE MOUNTAIN
RESCUE SERVICE
1960-1968

DUKE
HERO
OF THE
BLITZ
1936-1948

TEDDY
GOOD WITH SLIPPERS

'Four across is "Carpathian" ...'

'And when did you last see our supper?'

THE NINTH WONDER
OF THE WORLD

THE GREAT MONGREL
OF MANCHU

SIT !

'Rusty, do it like everyone else, will you!'